ChrisGoode

C000312050

monkey bars

by Chris Goode

Monkey Bars was first performed at the Traverse Theatre, Edinburgh on 14 August 2012

Cast: **Philip Bosworth**
       Angela Clerkin
       Jacquetta May
       Christian Roe
       Gwyneth Strong
       Gordon Warnecke

Writer / Director / Sound Design – **Chris Goode**
Dialogues originated by **Karl James**
Designer – **Naomi Dawson**
Lighting Designer – **Colin Grenfell**
Stage Manager / Tour Production Manager – **Helen Mugridge**
Producer – **Ric Watts**
Associate Designer – **Libby Todd**

For the Unicorn Theatre
Artistic Director – **Purni Morell**
Executive Director – **Anneliese Davidsen**
Programme Producer – **Carolyn Forsyth**
Technical Director – **Phil Clarke**
Technical Manager – **Andy Shewan**

A Chris Goode & Company and Unicorn Theatre co-production

Co-commissioned by Warwick Arts Centre and The Brewhouse Theatre & Arts Centre

Supported by the Jerwood Charitable Foundation

Developed with the support of the National Theatre Studio

ChrisGoodeandCompany

Thanks to: Shonagh Manson, Jon Opie and Alexis Stevens at Jerwood Charitable Trust; Paul Warwick, Ed Collier and Matt Burman at Warwick Arts Centre; Robert Miles at The Brewhouse; Orla O'Loughlin, Ruth McEwan, Ali Forbes and all at the Traverse; Matthew Poxon and all at National Theatre Studio; Lilli Geissendorfer at Arts Council England; Stephen Boxer, Lucy Ellinson and Alex Waldmann for their input into the research and development; Adam Brace, Laura McDermott and Ben Moor for their helpful and encouraging feedback; Maddy Costa; Alex Markham; Adam Mileusnic and Kevin Darton at Language; Richard Davenport; Giles Smart at United Agents; Dan Pursey and all at Mobius; and to all at Oberon Books.

ChrisGoodeandCompany

Chris Goode & Company is a new company formed by lead artist Chris Goode and producer Ric Watts to develop original collaborative and exploratory theatre projects across a variety of forms and contexts.

Chris Goode & Company provides a home for a broad range of (often uncategorisable) performance projects, principally focused on ensemble-based collaborative and participatory processes, and on formally innovative but accessible approaches to documentary and storytelling.

The company launched in March 2011 and fully realised projects to date include:

- **THE ADVENTURES OF WOUND MAN AND SHIRLEY**, a new version of Chris's acclaimed solo storytelling show for Edinburgh and BAC in 2011 and a UK Tour in 2012.
- **KEEP BREATHING**, a new solo interactive documentary performance about the science and ecology of breathing. A Drum Theatre Plymouth production, created with the support of London Word Festival, November 2011.
- **OPEN HOUSE**, an open-access and participatory week-long devising project, held at Transform at West Yorkshire Playhouse in June 2011, and at Mayfest, Bristol in May 2012.
- **GOD/HEAD**, an experimental documentary piece exploring the ambiguous interzone between religious faith and neuroscience. Made with Ovalhouse and Theatre in the Mill, February 2012.
- **9**, nine solo performances created by nine non-professional performers from Yorkshire in collaboration with the company, in co-production with West Yorkshire Playhouse, April 2012.

Whether in solo or group formats, the company's work is always collaboratively created by a fluid, constantly evolving ensemble of performers and makers, with Chris Goode's role as lead artist setting a characteristic tone of openness, friendliness and restless invention.

To find out more about **Chris Goode & Company**, and its work, past present and future, please visit www.chrisgoodeandcompany.co.uk or follow us on Twitter @chrisgoodeandco

UNICORN

THE UK'S LEADING THEATRE FOR YOUNG AUDIENCES

The Unicorn Theatre is the UK's leading theatre for young audiences, serving over 50,000 children, young people and families every year through its professional performances, participation and other events.

Founded in 1947 by Caryl Jenner, the company originally operated out of the back of a van, and touring theatre for children into schools and community centres. The Unicorn was subsequently based at the Arts Theatre in London's West End for many years, before moving into its current home at London Bridge in 2005. Today, the Unicorn building has two theatres, two rehearsal rooms and four floors of public space dedicated to producing and presenting work for audiences aged 2 to 21.

It is a central part of the Unicorn's mission to commission new work, to tour, to be accessible to all and to encourage exchange and collaboration between theatre-makers from different countries and traditions, coming together to develop ideas and projects.

unicorntheatre.com

Box Office 020 7645 0560
147 Tooley Street, London SE1 2HZ

Charity number: 225751
Company number 480920

Supported using public funding by
**ARTS COUNCIL
ENGLAND**

UNICORN

Artistic Director
Purni Morell
Executive Director
Anneliese Davidsen

ARTISTIC AND ADMINISTRATION
Programme Producer
Carolyn Forsyth
Finance Manager
Amanda Koch-Shick
Learning Associate
Catherine Greenwood
Learning and Participation Manager (Maternity Leave)
Ellen Edwin-Scott
Learning and Participation Manager (Maternity Leave)
Jenny Maddox
Learning and Participation Manager (Maternity Cover)
Ruth Weyman
General Administrator
Jenny Skene

DEVELOPMENT
Director of Development
Dorcas Morgan
Development Manager (Corporate Sponsorship)
Alex Jones
Development Manager (Trusts and Foundation)
(Maternity Leave) Marylka Gowlland
Development Manager (Trusts and Foundations)
(Maternity Cover) Caroline Darke
Development Officer
Melissa Wilkins

MARKETING & COMMUNICATIONS
Director of Marketing & Communications Nicki Marsh
Access Manager Kirsty Hoyle
Marketing Coordinator
Isabel Madgwick
Press and PR (freelance)
Cliona Roberts
Schools Relationship Manager
Ella MacFadyen
Front of House Manager
Sair Smith

Box Office Manager
Helen Corbett
Performance Managers
Lewis Church, Joycelyn Chung,
Laura Fiesco, Lyn Medcalf,
Laura Standen
Ushers Chris MaCallister,
Clare Quinn, Euan Borland,
Henry Reynolds, Housni Hassan,
Jackie Downer, Kathryn Tighe,
Krystal Boyde-Maynard, Laura
Standen, Lyn Medcalf,
Martin Walsh, Matthew Newell,
Miles Yekinni, Nadia Giscir, Nathan
Rumney, Phil Moore, Robert Weaver,
Thomas Dancaster
Box Office Assistants
Euan Borland, Laura Fiesco, Nadia
Giscir, Julia Hayes,
Phil Moore, Amy Mulholland, Clare
Quinn, Claire Sundin, Martin Walsh

TECHNICAL
Technical Director Phil Clarke
Technical Stage Manager
Andy Shewan
Stage Technician Jeff Mitchell
Sound Technician Keith Edgehill
Building Technician
Martin Turner
Lighting Technician Shane Burke
Stage Door Supervisors
Paul Brewster, John Cockerill,
Sidonie Ferguson, Alice Malseed

BOARD
Joanna Kennedy (Chair), Denise
Holle, Richard Hope, John Langley,
Carolyn Maddox, Bryan Savery,
Sarah West, Richard Oldfield.

YOUTH BOARD
Natalie Soobhee Nelson, Maria
Ratsevits, Kianna Witter-Prendergast,
Daniel Curthoys, Douglas Wood,
Florence Dessau

warwick arts centre

Warwick Arts Centre's programme is ambitious, confident, contemporary and international in perspective. Core to its mission is the nurturing of artistic partnerships with emerging, regional and international artists, characterised by their curiosity, originality and the ways in which their work engages with audiences.

Feeding directly into Warwick Arts Centre's commissioning strategy are two initiatives that have been developed in partnership with Associate Producers China Plate and which seek to support a spirit of adventure for both artists and audiences alike:

Triggered@Warwick Arts Centre is a commissioning and artist development programme that supports selected artists with time to develop creative ideas, physical space to work in, an audience to reflect on the work, dramaturgical and producing support and a commissioning fee. So far, Triggered@Warwick Arts Centre has supported projects by Mark Murphy, Caroline Horton, Contender Charlie, Greyscale, David Rosenberg, Reckless Sleepers and Action Hero.

Through the second commissioning strand, **This_Is_Tomorrow**, Warwick Arts Centre is seeking to develop new collaborative relationships between artists and academics at the University of Warwick. The project aims to engage selected artists in a meaningful way, connecting them with world-class academics, with the ultimate goal of creating projects across a range of practice and artform that express new research and thrilling discoveries to the widest possible audience.

www.warwickartscentre.co.uk

the brewhouse
theatre & arts centre

Located in Somerset's county town of Taunton, The Brewhouse Theatre & Arts Centre offers a varied programme of events for all ages including drama, dance, comedy, music, workshops, exhibitions and poetry.

The Brewhouse houses a 350 seat auditorium, two visual art exhibition spaces, an adaptable space for film and small scale performance, a creative space, and a Restaurant and Café Bar.

Our mission is to be a creative hub for the region, continually offering high quality experiences which entertain, stimulate, involve and inspire the many diverse communities we serve. We also provide an oasis for artists and creatives to meet and engage with the community through sharing of work, workshops, mentoring and participatory events. At the heart of what we do is the promotion of culture and the understanding of how it can enhance and enrich people's lives.

Alongside receiving touring productions and producing shows in-house, we regularly work in partnership and in collaboration with theatres and touring companies to ensure our audiences and communities get to see new work that has relevance to their lives.

The Brewhouse is delighted to co-commission *Monkey Bars*. What could be more universal than the voices of children? And in these difficult times we should be listening to the wisdom of the innocent. We're proud to be helping bring the show to the stage and letting Somerset audiences see the show in our studio space.

Artistic Director & Chief Executive **Robert Miles**

www.thebrewhouse.net

JERWOOD CHARITABLE FOUNDATION

The Jerwood Charitable Foundation is dedicated to imaginative and responsible revenue funding of the arts, supporting artists to develop and grow at formative stages in their careers. They work with artists across art forms, from dance and theatre to literature, music and the visual arts. For more information on the Jerwood Charitable Foundation visit:

www.jerwoodcharitablefoundation.org

PHILIP BOSWORTH

Recent projects: performer and designer for shadow puppet opera *The Adventures Of Thunder and Coal* (Nonesuch Theatre/Little Angel Theatre); puppet maker and operator for *Dickens' London*, a series of short films about The Life of Charles Dickens (BBC/Dan Films); co-devisor and performer for *Flogging A Dead Horse* (Faulty Optic/Potato Room Productions for London International Mime Festival and European tour); 'Henry' in the UK tour of Chris Goode's *Henry & Elizabeth* (Signal To Noise / Royal & Derngate); 'Henry's Dad' and 'Miss BattleAxe' in *Horrid Henry: Live and Horrid* (Sheffield Lyceum/Watershed, West End and UK Tour). Philip is also Associate Designer and performer with The Weirdy Beardies.

ANGELA CLERKIN

Angela previously worked with Chris Goode & Company in *Open House* at Bristol Mayfest and as a guest in *GOD/HEAD* (Ovalhouse). **Other theatre includes:** *Beauty & The Beast* (Lyceum); *Panic* (Sydney Opera House, Barbican); *Improbable's Lifegame* (National Theatre, Lyric, Bristol Old Vic, New York); *Bloody Chamber* (Northern Stage); *Seasons Greetings* (Liverpool); *Third Finger Left Hand* (Assembly Rooms); *Love and Other Fairy tales* (Pleasance); *Great Expectations* (Welsh Tour); *The Maids, Turn of the Screw* (Young Vic); *The Dream Killers* (Drill Hall); *Heartless, Belmer Darlings* (ICA); *Habeas Corpus* (Northampton); *Hedda Gabler, Shadow of a Gunman* (Leicester); *School For Wives* (Manchester); *The Government Inspector* (WYP); *A Flea In Her Ear* (Old Vic); *Gaudete* (Almeida). She supported The Pogues at Brixton Academy with Irish dance/comedy group *The Hairy Marys*. **TV includes:** *Holby City, Dalziel & Pascoe, My Family, EastEnders, Sugar Rush, All About George, Dean Spanley*, and *The Office*. Angela is also a writer. She is currently developing *The Bear* with Lee Simpson (an Improbable co-production) and *The Secret Keeper*, supported by the National Theatre Studio. Her screenplay *Head Over Heels* is under option with Spanish film company, A Contraluz. She has short stories published by Limehouse Books in *East* and *Men & Women*.

NAOMI DAWSON

Trained at Wimbledon School of Art and Kunstacademie, Maastricht. Previous work with Chris Goode includes: *Keep Breathing*, *King Pelican*, *Speed Death of the Radiant Child* (Drum Theatre, Plymouth); *Landscape and Monologue* (Ustinov, Bath); *...Sisters* (Gate/Headlong). **Other design includes:** *King John* (The Swan, RSC); *Mary Shelley* (Shared Experience, WYP and UK Tour); *Speechless* (Shared Experience, UK Tour); *Belongings* (Hampstead/Trafalgar Studios); *In Praise of Love* (Theatre Royal, Northampton); *Love and Money* (Malmo Stadsteater); *Amerika*, *Krieg der Bilder* (Staatstheater Mainz); *Scorched* (Dialogue/Old Vic Tunnels); *The Typist* (Sky Arts/Riverside Studios); *The Gods Weep* (RSC/Hampstead); *The Glass Menagerie* (Shared Experience/Salisbury Playhouse); *Rutherford and Son* (Northern Stage); *Three More Sleepless Nights* (Lyttelton, NT); *The Container* (Young Vic); *Can any Mother help me?* (Foursight/UK Tour); *Amgen: Broken* (Sherman Cymru); *If That's All There Is* (Lyric); *State of Emergency*, *Mariana Pineda* (Gate); *Stallerhof*, *Richard III*, *The Cherry Orchard*, *Summer Begins* (Southwark Playhouse); *Phaedra's Love* (Young Vic/Barbican Pit); *Different Perspectives* (Contact Theatre); *The Pope's Wedding*, *Forest of Thorns* (Young Vic); *Market Tales* (Unicorn); *Attempts on Her Life*, *Widows*, *Touched* (BAC); *In Blood*, *Venezuela*, *Mud*, *Trash*, *Headstone* (Arcola); *A Thought in Three Parts* (Burton Taylor). **Film credits include:** costume design for short film *Love After a Fashion*, set design for *Fragile* by Idris Khan.

CHRIS GOODE

Chris Goode is a writer, director, performer and sound designer, who has been described as "one of the most exciting talents working in Britain today" (*Guardian*) and "an extremely highly regarded alternative theatre maker" (Caroline McGinn, *Time Out*). His work has included two Fringe First award-winning shows: *Neutrino* (with Unlimited Theatre: Soho Theatre, London, and international tour), and his own solo debut *Kiss of Life* (Pleasance, Edinburgh; Drill Hall, London), which in 2007 travelled to Sydney Opera House as part of the Sydney International Festival. In 2008 he won the inaugural Headlong/Gate New Directions Award for his production *...Sisters* at the Gate Theatre. More recently he was part of the international touring cast of Tim Crouch's controversial and acclaimed play *The Author*, winner of the John Whiting Award and a Total Theatre Award for Innovation.

Other notable recent work has included: *9* (West Yorkshire Playhouse); *GOD/HEAD* (Ovalhouse and Theatre in the Mill); *Open House* (West Yorkshire Playhouse and Mayfest); *The Adventures of Wound Man and Shirley* (BAC and UK tour); *Keep Breathing* (London Word Festival and Drum Theatre Plymouth); *The Loss of All Things* (as part of Sixty-Six Books at the Bush); a trilogy, *Who You Are* (Tate Modern); *Where You Stand* (Contact Theatre, Manchester) and *Where We Meet* (site-responsive, Edinburgh); *Glass House* (Royal Opera House Covent Garden); *Landscape and Monologue* (Ustinov, Bath); *Hey Mathew* (Theatre in the Mill, Bradford); *King Pelican* and *Speed Death of the Radiant Child* (Drum Theatre, Plymouth); *Longwave* (Lyric, Hammersmith). Chris's *The History of Airports: Selected texts for performance 1995-2009* was published in 2009 by Ganzfeld. As a poet he has published three chapbooks with Barque Press, and he has recently edited *Better Than Language: An anthology of new modernist poetries* for Ganzfeld.

COLIN GRENFELL

Recent theatre includes: *The Steamie* (25th Anniversary Tour); *The Caretaker* (Liverpool Everyman/Trafalgar Studios/World Tour); *Horse Piss for Blood* (Plymouth Drum); *Hansel and Gretel* (Glasgow Citizens); *The Village Social* (National Theatre of Wales); *Tartuffe* (ETT); *Macbeth* (Liverpool Everyman); *Pandas* (Traverse); *Piccard in Space* (Southbank Centre); *Faith and Cold Reading* (Live Theatre); *Canary* (Liverpool Playhouse/ETT/Hampstead); *Through a Glass Darkly*, *When the Rain Stops Falling* (Almeida Theatre); *The Glass Menagerie* (Salisbury Playhouse/ Shared Experience); *Steel Magnolias*, *A Doll's House*, *Equus* (Dundee Rep); *The Beauty Queen of Leenane* (Edinburgh Lyceum); *I Am Yusuf and This is my Brother* (Young Vic); *Men Should Weep*, *365*, *The Bacchae*, *Black Watch* (National Theatre of Scotland); *Single Spies* (Theatre Royal Bath Productions); *Riflemind* (Trafalgar Studios); *Alex* (Arts Theatre); *No Idea*, *Panic*, *Theatre of Blood*, *Spirit*, *The Hanging Man*, *Lifegame*, *Coma*, *Animo*, *70 Hill Lane* (Improbable); *Baby Baby* (Stellar Quines); *Kes*, *Separate Tables* (Royal Exchange Manchester); *Touched* (Salisbury Playhouse); *Enjoy* (Watford Palace Theatre); *Unprotected* (Liverpool Everyman); *Casanova*, *Playing the Victim* (Told by an Idiot). **Opera includes:** extensive work for Opera Holland Park, *Falstaff* (Mid-Wales Opera); *Fidelio* (Opera Touring Company Dublin); *La Bohème* (English Touring Opera) and *The Thief of Baghdad* (Royal Opera House).

KARL JAMES

As director of The Dialogue Project, most of Karl's time is spent helping people have conversations when the stakes are high. His work as a dialogue artist involves recording, editing and publishing conversations on themes sometimes considered difficult to talk about. His series *Intimate Conversations* is available online and has been a highlight of Latitude Festival since 2005. Founded by Karl in response to the events of 9/11, The Dialogue Project enables powerful and productive conversations, bringing together people with different points of view to help them co-create ideas, solutions and resolution. As a mediator,

facilitator and speaker, Karl helps individuals, teams and boards to connect more deeply through dialogue, working with a wide range of organisations, businesses and charities from global giants like Unilever to smaller set-ups like Arrival Education and the Architectural Association. Karl occasionally resurrects his theatre work to direct the plays of Tim Crouch with co-director Andy Smith. *My Arm*, *An Oak Tree*, *England* and most recently *The Author* have enjoyed success in the UK and abroad. Karl's first book on conversation will be published by Pearson in 2013 and his first series for BBC Radio 4 will be broadcast this Autumn. www.thedialogueproject.com
www.understandingdifference.blogspot.com

JACQUETTA MAY

Theatre includes: *Neaptide*, *A Matter of Life and Death* and *Schism In England* (Royal National Theatre); *Comedy of Errors* and *Little Murders* (Manchester Royal Exchange); *Lady Chatterley's Lover* (Derby Playhouse); *Crimes of the Heart* (Liverpool Playhouse); *Twelfth Night* and *The Browning Version* (Belgrade Theatre Coventry); *Abigail's Party* (Colchester Mercury); *Albertine in Five Times* (BAC); *Educating Rita* (Theatre Gwynedd); *Stealing Sweets and Punching People* (Theatre503/Latchmere); *The Memory of Water* (Watford Palace). **TV:** Jacquetta has been a regular in *EastEnders* (Rachel Kominski), *Cardiac Arrest*, *Home Farm Twins* for 2 series each, and *Dangerfield*. She has also appeared in *Being Human*, *Silent Witness*, *New Tricks*, *Law and Order*, *I'm Still Alan Partridge*, *Cold Feet*, *Uncle Silas*, *Four Fathers*, *Holby City*, *Crocodile Shoes* and many others. **Film:** *Naked Call*, *Get Real*. **As a scriptwriter** Jacquetta is currently working on two BBC commissions (with Ruby Films and Twenty Twenty) and a three parter for ITV Studios about a poltergeist. Her film *In Love With Barbara* has been shown many times on BBC4, she adapted *Fear of Flying* by Erica Jong for Mammoth Screen and Sundance Channel (U.S) and has written episodes for *Where The Heart Is*, *New Tricks*, *No Angels*, *Personal Affairs* and *Torchwood*. She co-created *Ugetme* for CBBC which ran to 3 series. Jacquetta co-founded and co-ran the new writing theatre company

Plain Clothes Productions, commissioning and developing scripts for national tours and runs at BAC, Young Vic, The Bush and The Traverse. She directed *Her Sister's Tongue* at The Lyric Theatre Hammersmith.

HELEN MUGRIDGE

Helen is an experienced stage and production manager. Her previous credits include: *Mass Observation*, Inspector Sands (Almeida); *Cooking Ghosts*, Beady Eye (Currently in development); *Penumbra*, Indefinite Articles (The Roundhouse and Norwich Puppet Theatre); *BYO*, Thickskin (Research and development); *2401 Objects*, Analogue (Edinburgh, national and European tour); *The Adventures of Wound Man and Shirley*, Chris Goode & Company (Edinburgh); *Total Football*, Ridiculusmus (Barbican Pit and Belfast Festival); *Beachy Head*, Analogue (National and European tour); *Poetry for Morons*, Arlette George (Edinburgh); *Everything Must Go*, Beady Eye/ Kristin Fredrickson (National and European Tour); *The Poof Downstairs*, Jon Haynes (National tour); *Shoot/ Get Treasure/Repeat* and *Eshara*, Cheekish Productions (National tour); *Special*, fecund theatre (Edinburgh); *The Gruffalo*, Tall Stories (Soho Theatre and International tour); *Hello You*, fecund theatre (Riverside Studios); *Say Nothing* and *Ideas Men*, Ridiculusmus (Barbican Pit); *Jungle* (BAC) and *Don Q* (Edinburgh Festival), Labyrinth Theatre.

CHRISTIAN ROE

Christian trained at LAMDA and the National Youth Theatre. Since graduating **theatre includes:** *Roaring Trade* (Paines Plough/Soho Theatre); *The Power of Yes* (National Theatre); *Sixty-Six Books* (Bush Theatre). **Television includes:** *Wallander*, *Walter's War*, *Criminal Justice*, *White Heat* (BBC).

GWYNETH STRONG

Theatre includes: Celia in *A Round-Healed Woman* (Aldwych Theatre); Ruth in *Von Ribbentrop's Watch* (Oxford Playhouse); Kath Casey in *Our House* (Birmingham Rep and UK tour); *Celebrating Linda Smith* (UK Tour); Carol in *Girls Night* (Milton Keynes Theatre); Angela in *When You Cure Me* (Bush); The Other Woman in *Take A Chance on Me* (New End); Kitty in *Ancient Lights* (Hampstead); Masha in *Three Sisters* (Out of Joint); *A Piece of Mind* (Nuffield, Southampton and Apollo); *Care* (Royal Court); Maria in *Woyzeck* (Lyric Hammersmith); Carol in *Sugar and Space* (Royal Court) and Christine in *Shout Across the River* (RSC/Warehouse). **Film includes:** *Suzie Gold*, *Crimetime*, *Cry Freedom* and *Bloody Kids*. **Television includes:** *Midsomer Murders*, *New Tricks*, *Murder in Suburbia*, *Casualty*, *Only Fools and Horses*, *Harry Enfield's Brand Spanking New Show*, *Real Women*, *Lucy Sullivan is Getting Married*, *An Unsuitable Job For A Woman*, *Forgotten*, *A Touch of Frost*, *The Missing Postman*, *Silent Witness*, *Nice Town*, *99-1*, *Clothes in the Wardrobe*, *King of the Ghetto* and *Rainy Day Woman*.

GORDON WARNECKE

Trained at De Lean Drama School. He played the co-lead opposite Daniel Day Lewis in *My Beautiful Laundrette*. **Other film work includes:** Franco Zeffirelli's *Young Toscanini*. *London Kills Me*, *The Pleasure Principle*, *Looking For You*, *A Nice Arrangement*, *Exitz* and *The Telemachy* (due for release in 2013). **TV credits include:** *Boon*, *EastEnders*, *The Bill*, *Brookside*, *Only Fools And Horses*, *Birds Of A Feather*, *Dr Who*, *A Fatal Inversion* by Barbara Vine and *Y Pris*. **Theatre includes:** *Julius Caesar*, *The Jew Of Malta*, *Bite Of The Night* directed by Danny Boyle and *The Will* all for The Royal Shakespeare Company, *Blood* at The Royal Court Theatre, *Borderline* at the Nuffield Theatre, *A Christmas Carol* and *Cinderella* at Trinity Theatre and a National tour of Ibsen's *An Enemy Of The People* for Tara Arts playing Peter Stockman. He wrote and directed his first short film *The Magician*, which was released in April 2012. His second short *Whispers* is due for release in October 2012.

RIC WATTS

Ric Watts is an independent producer based in Manchester, and a co-founder of Chris Goode & Company, for whom he has produced all of the company's major work to date. Ric is also Producer for Unlimited Theatre (resident company at West Yorkshire Playhouse) for whom he has produced *Mission To Mars*, *The Ethics of Progress* and *The Giant & The Bear*, alongside developing new shows, including *Money the game show* and *The Noise*; and Analogue, for whom he has produced *Mile End*, *Beachy Head*, *Lecture Notes on a Death Scene*, *Living Film Set* and *2401 Objects* in Edinburgh and on UK Tour. He started his career as Producer at Your Imagination, where he produced work by Cartoon de Salvo, Ridiculusmus and Kazuko Hohki. Since 2006, Ric has been working independently, with notable successes including: *FOOD* by theimaginarybody; *Particularly in the Heartland* by The TEAM; *FIT* by Rikki Beadle-Blair for Queer Up North; *The Adventures of Wound Man and Shirley* by Chris Goode in co-production with Queer Up North; *Twelfth Night* with Filter Theatre and Schtanhaus; *Paperweight* and *Free Time Radical* by The Frequency D'ici; *Running on Air* by Laura Mugridge; *Flathampton* for Royal & Derngate and *Avon Calling* by The Other Way Works. Ric was also the Festival Producer for the 2010 Queer Up North International Festival.

LISTEN TO ME

"You're lucky" said Tobias, aged 8. "Everyone's listening to you."

And yes, Tobias. I am lucky. I'm lucky enough to be listened to. Sometimes.

But when I sit with Tobias and the other children at Educare Small School in Kingston as I do on the occasional Monday morning to run what's become known as Listening Circle, my intention isn't really to be listened to. It's to listen. And to listen well.

On those mornings I pay conscious attention to how I listen, just as I would when I'm recording an intimate conversation with someone on the subject of pain or sex or when I'm mediating between opposing groups of people in a hot and dusty tent somewhere or facilitating a conversation with board members of a global business. The situations may change - but the skills remain the same.

So in my role on *Monkey Bars* (which was simply to record conversations with children and then hand them over to Chris for transcribing) I did nothing new or special. I did what I always try to do. I employed as gracefully as I can the ten core skills of dialogue at the service of as rich a conversation as possible.

So when each child walked into the private space we'd organised, before I got them to press the red button marked REC, we'd address an important question together; the question that ought really to be asked before every conversation: Why are we having this conversation?

It's the question that's on every child's lips as they walk into the room and it's a question that draws to the surface one of the most important ingredients of a dialogue: shared intent. My answer to this question would normally be something like this: "Well – usually a project starts with an idea. And behind this project is an idea that sometimes children aren't always listened to."

"Do you find that sometimes?" I'd ask. A nod of the head would often follow; sometimes quite a fervent nodding of the head. I'd tell them that our conversation would never be 'heard' as recorded, but instead it might become source material for a script. "A script for a piece of theatre that puts the words of children into the mouths of adults."

"What do you think?" I would ask.

"Why are you doing that?" they'd want to know. "Well, because I think Chris suspects that one reason why children's voices aren't always heard is that people don't really take children seriously. And that maybe by hearing what you say through other people standing on a stage - not other children but other adults - maybe people might listen differently to what you have to say."

"Okay" they often replied, but this time with a slower more thoughtful look on their face. (Any other comments at this stage were usually confined to just one word: "Interesting.")

I'd then make clear to the children that if they found themselves saying anything on tape that they'd rather not have used then they should say so and that would be fine; we wouldn't use it. (None of them did.)

Then I'd tell them that the only thing I'd really ask of them was to be as honest as they could be. And in return I would assure them that they weren't about to be judged or assessed by me or Chris. "This isn't a test, it's a conversation." I'd say.

And so we'd start talking.

And I'd start listening: *to, for, from* and *with*.

I'd listen *to* the content of what they had to say.

I'd listen *for* the small clues that lie within and behind the content, the tiny hints that might be worth exploring more.

And I'd acknowledge where I was listening *from*: a position of adult curiosity – as an outsider if you like. (How could I be anything but an outsider? I'm an adult after all.)

And sometimes – and only sometimes – I'd get close to listening *with* these young people; occasionally finding myself trusted enough to be allowed to sit with them as it were and glimpse through their eyes and ears how the world might seem to be.

It's this final layer of listening – empathic listening – that I find the most challenging of all, no matter who I'm having a conversation with. Why? Because it's so tempting to kid myself that I'm already doing it. It's easy to tell ourselves that "we really understand what it's like" for someone who's had an entirely individual experience. It gives us a warm glow to imagine that we can truly share someone else's point of view; that we can actually sit in their position and feel what something must have been like for them. But truly, this is much harder than we think. Empathy-lite is common; genuine empathy is rare. And so the moment I begin to utter the words 'that must have been amazing' or 'scary' or 'thrilling' or 'upsetting for you', I know I'm probably in a dangerous place, because I'm probably in the wrong place. I'm painting *their* picture with *my* brush, with my palette and my experience of life. And in doing so I've hijacked the conversational journey. As we all do. As we often do.

So, in order to do my best to co-create a healthy conversation, I'll employ the skills of dialogue, my everyday working tools. I'll check rather than assume. I'll dig deeper before I challenge or query. I'll make sure we're both okay with where we are and where we're going. I'll encourage them to describe their experience using personal and specific examples rather than abstract or broad generalisations. I'll walk the talk of dialogue as gently and as generously as I can. But, as essential as a set of well-defined and sharp tools may be, it's not enough. And like all the other skills of dialogue, listening well is about a lot more than efficiency and good practice.

Good listening is about attitude; something that's hard to teach, but simple to explain. For me it's as simple as this: behind every good listener is a desire to hear.

In my experience, if there's anything that can be trusted to make a real difference to a conversation it's that: the presence of desire. It's curiosity that creates the space for a bigger conversation and transforms what could be just an interview into a dialogue.

It's not always easy to be curious. But when you're sitting with a 9-year-old, personally it comes naturally. I'm curious about what they think. I'm curious to hear how they're beginning to construct their perspective on the world. And I'm curious to find out whether being listened to is the norm or the exception.

So I'd like to thank the children and their teachers and parents for talking part in this project. I'd like to thank them for talking to me and for answering my questions. And I'd like to thank them for being curious enough to sometimes ask me some good questions too.

As one child said to me at the end of a conversation: "it's nice to have someone be interested really."

Karl James

A NOTE ON THE TEXT

The script of *Monkey Bars* is distilled from transcripts of over eleven hours of recorded private conversations between dialogue artist Karl James and a total of 72 children aged between six and eleven, from a wide range of social, cultural and geographical backgrounds but all currently living in or near London. Mostly Karl talked to the children in pairs; some were one-to-one conversations; and in a couple of cases, two children were recorded speaking together without Karl being present.

As the play text indicates, the children were all aware of the context in which these conversations were being recorded and the use that might eventually be made of their words – as were their parents and teachers.

The text is strictly verbatim and the only editorial interventions made have been in selecting the excerpts to be used, and sometimes reducing the children's (and Karl's) words, and/or reordering sequences of dialogue, for the sake of clarity. Not one word has been added or altered, with the necessary exception that all names have been changed.

The makers of *Monkey Bars* would like to extend their warmest thanks to the participating schools for their hospitality and support, and, of course, to all the children themselves – those who are represented in the final text and those who aren't – for the great generosity of their candour, their insights and their incredible imaginations.

Monkey Bars is affectionately dedicated to the memory of Mike Drew, who died while the show was in development, and who, throughout his professional and personal life, elevated to a fine art the radical practice of listening to children and daring to take them seriously.

Chris Goode

MONKEY BARS

OBERON BOOKS
LONDON

WWW.OBERONBOOKS.COM

First published in 2012 by Oberon Books Ltd
521 Caledonian Road, London N7 9RH
Tel: +44 (0) 20 7607 3637 / Fax: +44 (0) 20 7607 3629
e-mail: info@oberonbooks.com
www.oberonbooks.com

A catalogue record for this book is available from the British Library.

PB ISBN: 978-1-84943-469-0
E ISBN: 978-1-84943-588-8

Cover design: Language
Cover photography: Richard Davenport

Printed and bound by Marston Book Services Limited, Didcot.

Visit www.oberonbooks.com to read more about all our books
and to buy them. You will also find features, author interviews and
news of any author events, and you can sign up for e-newsletters
so that you're always first to hear about our new releases.

This text went to press before the end of rehearsals
and so may differ slightly from the play as performed.

1.

A boy sits patiently, quietly singing to his jelly.

Another boy blows up a balloon. He lets it go and watches happily as it flies around in mid-air.

Six smartly-dressed adults come one by one into the room. The boys disappear.

2.

KARL   OK. So my name's Karl, and let me tell you a little bit about what we're doing here, shall I? Er, I'm working with a man called Chris who's making a play, and the idea behind the play is that sometimes adults don't really listen to children. How... What do you think about that? Do you think that's true? Do you think adults sometimes don't listen to you?

KIM   *(Weird snoring sound.)*

JACOB   Sometimes.

KARL   Sometimes. – What do you think?

KIM   Sometimes yeah.

KARL   Yeah. So we might talk about that in a minute. So Chris is going to take conversations between children just like you and then he's going to put them into his play, but they'll be spoken not by children but by...?

KIM   Adults!

KARL   So the adults will be speaking the children's words. And we'll see if the audience think that's interesting. What do you think about that?

HOLLY   Wow!

KIM   *(Nods.)*

HOLLY   I never had a… I never, um, had my voice in a grown-up's voice.

SULAIMAN   Yeah.

KARL   Good. *(Coughs.)* So I'm only telling you that so that you know what's happening.

REUBEN   Is this a real microphone?

KARL   Yeah.

JACK   *(Trying the mic.)* One. Two. Three. Four. Five. Six. Seven. Eight. Nine. Ten.

KARL   Yeah. That's how it works.

NEIL   *(Joining in at the mic.)* Eleven. *(Laughs.)*

KARL   We can stop now! *(Laughs.)*

NEIL   Twelve. Thirteen. Fourteen.

KARL   Excellent, all right.

NEIL   Fifteen hundred and twenty-six.

KARL   OK. – So it takes your voice and puts it inside the machine.

JACK   So it's like…the speed of sound.

KARL   It travels at the speed of sound. It certainly does. Do you know about the speed of sound?

JACK   Yeah… – I know what the expression of "speed of a sound" the figure of speech what it is.

KARL   OK.

CLAIRE   This is so cool.

KARL   So the idea really is for us to talk about a few things and for me to hear about what you think. So if I put like a subject on the table and then you can talk about it, how do you feel about that?

WOODY   Hm. OK.

3.

ALICE   Um, well, I live opposite a park, which is really good, and I normally just go, like, there with my friends, and we just normally just go in the bushes and, like, talk a bit – and it's just nice and quiet where no one would disturb you or anything.

You wouldn't notice cos it's like a main road thing. You just wouldn't notice a park would be there.

It's always quiet.

It's quite nice.

Cos when you know where it's, like, where everybody knows a park's there… When you see it you think, oh yeah, that looks good, I might go in there, and it just gets really busy, and you think, oh, I wish I knew, like, a different place where no one knew anything, or…anyone would know that there's like a park there.

So it's quite good that I live opposite a park that's nice and quiet.

4.

ROSCOE   I was hanging by one arm off, like, a chairlift.

And it was still moving. So I sort of had to like… But I couldn't get the other arm up.

Cos if I did then I'd probably lose the grip on one arm… Cos like ski gloves aren't grippy. And then I couldn't…

And then finally my dad, like, lifted me up. He just lifted me up.

So it was, like, swinging. And my dad was lifting me up.

It was so sc- … Cos it was like halfway through the chairlift, so it was so high.

I was sort of…calm but… My mum, cos she was screaming…

So, like, I was sort of panicking cos of she was panicking.

It was literally just ice.

5.

A wine bar. Tinkly piano music. Towards the end of the evening.

EDEN   The thing that makes me sad is when I have like nightmares. One time I had a really scary nightmare. *(Laughs.)* Of a monster was chasing me.

JOAQUIN   *(Laughs.)*

EDEN   My mum got took away! And I woke up and I just started crying! *(Laughs.)*

JOAQUIN   Um, the thing that makes me sad is when…I have to wake up very early.

EDEN   One time I woke up at like four o'clock or something because I had to go with my dad to work.

JOAQUIN   I was nearly up till midnight with my mum.

EDEN   Woah.

JOAQUIN   Because she was tidying up my bed.

EDEN   One time I stayed up till three o'clock. At my nanny's house. She lets me sleep late.

JOAQUIN   I'm allowed… I'm allowed to sleep up. When, when I'm, when I'm, when it's half-term.

EDEN   Oh yeah. Every night my mum just said "Go to sleep" at seven o'clock, and I was like, Nooo! *(Laughs.)* It's half-term! I can go to sleep at midnight or whatever I want!

            My big brother goes to, goes to sleep at five o'clock. Because he goes college, and he has to wake up like really early at six. Yeah and, um, when he has to wake up, he doesn't wake up, so my mum just said… Come… Come and slap him on the face! *(Laughs.)*

JOAQUIN   Or… pour water on them.

EDEN   Yeah, or… just, on his face, just go like that. *(Knocks on the table.)*

JOAQUIN   Or pour water.

EDEN   *(Laughs.)* Yeah!

JOAQUIN   A cold water to wake them up.

EDEN   Yeah one time, one time I thought, I thought it was cold water yeah but it was actually boiling hot so…he got burn marks everywhere. *(Laughs.)*

            Quiet.

JOAQUIN   My mum… My mum sometimes dreams that she's gone smaller. To a normal age. Gone smaller.

EDEN   How do you know she dreams about that? You can't see dreams.

JOAQUIN   Because she always she always she always tells me, every morning. She says what she dreamed about, and I said, I dream about something, too.

EDEN   And what is that dream?

JOAQUIN   Um…there was a blue bee chasing me.

EDEN   There's a what?

JOAQUIN   A bee.

EDEN   *(Laughs.)* That's quite funny.

JOAQUIN   It was scared me. I don't want to wake up.

EDEN   *(Laughs.)* Well you have to.

JOAQUIN   Because I was scared from the bee. …Because it was blue.

EDEN   Well you have to wake up to make the dream go away and then you're never ever going to see that dream again.

JOAQUIN   Yeah but I was deep in my sleep so I couldn't wake up. Unless my mum woke me up.

EDEN   What like Sleeping Beauty?

JOAQUIN   Yes.

EDEN   *(Laughs.)*

6.

KARL   What do you think you'll be like when you're a grown-up?

JAMAAL   Tall.

KARL   Really?

JAMAAL   Yeah.

KARL   OK.

JAMAAL   I think I'll be strong as well.

KARL   Strong and tall. OK. And what kind of a job would you like to do?

JAMAAL   Er… Superhero.

KARL   A superhero! And, um, what about you, Stevie?

STEVIE   I'll be strong, tough and tall and big…and…I'll
              be *so* strong.

KARL   Would you really?

STEVIE   Yeah.

JAMAAL   I would be more stronger than that. …Or both
              be the same strongness.

KARL   You could both be the same amount of strong.

JAMAAL   Mm.

DEANNE   When I was younger I used to wonder what my
              job would be, and I used to, like, have a list, with
              all the jobs that I'd like to do. But then now, I
              don't like any of them. Like, I wrote down once,
              I remember, actor, or, like, pop star. *(Laughs.)*

ESTHER   I used to walk in my mum's shoes and think
              what job I would like to be when I'm older.

CAREY   What would you do when you're an adult?

GRACE   Um… Um… Maybe I'll be a actor or a cupcake
              lady.

OMAR   Yeah, I'm gonna, I'm gonna be a police officer.

RACHID   It's kind of dangerous!

OMAR   OK then… A…a…ones where you walk on
              people's backs. OK then.

RACHID   Massage.

OMAR   Yeah massage. No. No. A doctor that walks on
              people's backs.

RACHID   Oh oh oh yeah OK. Like when you work in the
              back of the bones.

MATTHEW   This, um, fortune teller said that I was going to
              become an astronaut, but I think that's highly…
              impossible.

33

OMAR	No. No. No, 'scuse me. I'm going to be an ambience actually. A middle one that carries the beds up into the front.
SID	I am not sure if I'll be, like, a tramp, or –
ZACHARY	*(Laughs.)* Or a super-guy.
SID	Yeah, or a, or a banker or something. – Well they're the same thing, but…
	(Everyone laughs.)
KARL	What do you think the best thing is about being an adult? When you look at adults, what do you think, oh that will be brilliant?
KIERAN	Having a beard.
KARL	Having a beard?
KIERAN	I would just like to…stroke my beard. Like…
DEXTER	Yeah! You could just comb it every day and it'd be…
KIERAN	Drooping down…
DEXTER	Drooping down your body and just trailing behind you. *(Laughs.)*
KARL	What are the things you think, oh no, that must be awful, when you're an adult?
DEXTER	Um… When, like, when you're, like, addicted to things, like smoking and beer and things like that.
KARL	Do you think addiction is a bad thing?
DEXTER	It depends what you're addicted to.
KARL	Right.
DEXTER	Like, you could be addicted to, um…er… Messing with electricity, which is bad.

LAKEISHA	My mum said if you're a…, when you're a kid you want to be an adult, but when you're an adult you want to go…back to be a kid.
KARL	*(Laughs.)* Really? Do you think that's true?
LAKEISHA	Well, I don't know.
KARL	Do you think about going to secondary school much?
ELINA	Yeah. I don't actually want to. I don't want to go in a school with boys cos there are stories where they, where they beat up people. And that's a bit disturbing. *(Laughs.)*
	Beat.
DEXTER	*(Laughs.)* "He's got his beard dangling down again!"

7.

A marquee at a small-town literary festival.

JULIETTE	Well I really like writing stories and I like making up characters and things.
KARL	Ah, do you? Where do you get those stories and characters from?
JULIETTE	Probably from things I do or see.
KARL	Really?
JULIETTE	Yeah.
KARL	Could you give me an example? What's something that you've written recently where you've…
JULIETTE	Well, sometimes I see kids playing in the park and I, like, write about, like, what it would be like if they were, like, actually on their own in the park.

KARL | Do you, are you a very observant type of person, do you think?

JULIETTE | Sort of. Yeah.

KARL | What kinds of things do you notice when you watch people?

JULIETTE | Um… Well, the, like, sort of things they're playing and like what they're playing and things.

KARL | Mm. How interesting! …What kind of stories do you enjoy writing?

JULIETTE | Fiction, like, um, adventure stories.

KARL | What's, what's the story that you're most proud of writing so far? Is there one particular piece of work that you're proud of?

JULIETTE | Um… Well I've done lots so I'm not sure, but… Probably this one about some children in the park, like I said, that I got the idea from. And they all like get lost in the park or something.

KARL | OK.

JULIETTE | I think. Yeah, I didn't, I started it recently, so…

KARL | OK.

JULIETTE | I think it's quite good.

8.

FRAN, throwing and catching a tennis ball.

KARL | What do you do when you're cross?

FRAN | —

KARL | Do you throw things around, or… What do you do?

FRAN | I go to my room and I get a tennis ball and throw it on the wall, catch it, and throw it again.

KARL	What, how long do you do that for?
FRAN	Till I feel a bit better.
KARL	Really? Do you?
FRAN	Mm. Sometimes.
KARL	Did you invent that way of calming down? Did you just do that one day?
FRAN	Yep.
KARL	And does it work?
FRAN	…Sometimes.

9.

JACK	I went down a hill on my bike…
	Done a front skid. Done a front wheelie. Went head first. Had a big scar on my face.
	Lucky it was on Hallowe'en!

10.

KARL	. . .Those are headphones to listen to your voices.
RACHID	Oh, they're like like when you go to a studio.
KARL	Exactly. Exactly. So are you two interested in music?
OMAR	No!
RACHID	No! It's *haraam* for us.
KARL	It's what for you?
RACHID	Haraam.
OMAR	We are Muslims actually.

RACHID   We're not allowed to hear music because our, it's like a rule for our God.

OMAR   We are not allowed to say the T-word.

RACHID   Yeah.

KARL   …OK. So don't say the T-word. I don't know what it is but you don't need to say it.

OMAR   It's… Can I say the…bit?

RACHID   Yeah. A bit. *(Laughs.)*

OMAR   C… R…

RACHID   …You can say the whole thing you know. It's cool.

OMAR   OK. – What, can you?

RACHID   Yeah. It's cool.

OMAR   'Cross.'

KARL   Cross?

OMAR   Yeah.

RACHID   Yeah. – That starts with a 'C'.

OMAR   Oh.

KARL   What, you can't say 'cross'?

RACHID   Yeah.

KARL   Why can't you say 'cross'? It's just a word, isn't it.

RACHID   No because it's the Christian cross and we're not Christian. It's haraam for us.

KARL   Mm. So what do you think about Christians? Do they feel like very different people to you?

RACHID   Yes!

OMAR   Like… No, I'm not allowed to say it… They're crazy.

KARL   *(Laughs.)*

OMAR   Well yes they are.

KARL   Do you think?

OMAR   Yeah cos they smoke. They are crazy.

RACHID   We're not allowed to smoke.

OMAR   And beer! Yeah. They drink beer every day.

RACHID   Yeah. And get drunk and die quicker. So yeah.

OMAR   No. No. Just move around and do funny stuff.

KARL   Mm. – Religion is very important to you, isn't
            it? You have a faith don't you. You have a
            Muslim faith.

OMAR   Is it playtime? No?

KARL   No, not playtime yet.

OMAR   It's like, do not lie, or you will get more…down
            points.

RACHID   Yeah. If you do good things, you might, you're
            gonna go heaven. But if you do bad things,
            you're going to go near to hell-fire.

OMAR   Um, this is the thing. Muslims can't lie, but the,
            um, but the other people that are not Muslims,
            they can lie as much as they want and they
            won't go anywhere. So.

KARL   Do you ever meet people who think that you're
            wrong, who disagree with your faith, who don't
            believe in hell and things like that?

RACHID   Oh oh um they're called atheists or something.
            We have a teacher. He learns year four. He's a
            atheist. He was in year three before. Now he
            went to year four he doesn't believe in nothing.

KARL   And do you think that's OK?

RACHID   No.

KARL   Why…

RACHID   Like if you just change to another subject like.

OMAR   Can I play the guitar?

KARL   No, not now, no.

RACHID   Basically… They should believe in something.

OMAR   Some people don't pray.

RACHID   That's Christians.

OMAR   Yeah. They don't pray. And they don't care
            whatever they do cos they're not bothered. …
            What? They are not bothered! To do anything!

RACHID   OK! So let's go to a different subject!

11.

Round a table in the staff canteen.

RACHEL   Would you like to be famous?

CRESSIDA   Yeah. I want to feel what it's like to be famous
            for one day.

RACHEL   Yeah. Well I love it but apart from the fact how
            you have to like…

CRESSIDA   …cope with paparazzi or something.

RACHEL   Yeah and you can't like… If like when we go to
            get some milk like it's all right if you just run in
            your sneakers and your pyjamas. With a decent
            jumper on. Like if you're literally going to the
            corner shop. You have to put on your make-up
            and have like fully everything, just to go down
            to the corner shop. Which I think is quite sad
            really.

CRESSIDA   They should be able to get their own personal
            space.

RACHEL   And really like… I've forgotten, was it Katy
          Perry that's going to not be famous any more?
          Lily Allen, that's it. Like, she's, she doesn't want
          to be famous, but, like, she's always going to
          be famous, whatever happens, like, people are
          going to be like, wow, it's Lily Allen. You know?

NADIA   I think I'm gonna be famous! *(Laughs.)*

RUTH   That's what I think about myself! I think about
          the things that will happen to me when…if I
          become famous, all that stuff. I don't think about
          the bad thing of it, I think about the good thing
          of it.

NADIA   But I also plan like…what would happen if I'm
          not famous.

RUTH   That's a good plan.

NADIA   Cos like I want to be a singer, but like if I don't
          become famous then I want to be a teacher, or
          um…

RUTH   You have like a back-up plan.

NADIA   Yeah.

RUTH   If I become famous I don't want to be by myself.
          I want to be in a band.

NADIA   Yeah.

RUTH   So like if some of them hate me, they wouldn't
          just hate me, they would hate the band as well.
          – If you're like one person they would just like
          "Oh I hate you, look at her" and like they would
          concentrate on you, but if you are a band they
          wouldn't just hate you, they would hate the
          other people, so you wouldn't be that sad and
          like…

NADIA   Yeah but sometimes the bandmate can hate you
          as well. Like in the Pussycat Dolls. Sometimes

yeah like they hate like one specific member of the band. Like me as well. I hate one specific, um, girl from a band.

KARL   What do you think it's like, if you're in a band and you know that some of you have got more talent than others? Because sometimes those things are really obvious, aren't they?

RUTH   Yeah. Well I wouldn't point it out to them. I would just, like, courage them. Like tell them they brave and that stuff. Instead of saying, "Oh, you're rubbish, of course they hate you." I think that you should not criticize some of your friends. Like.

TAMEKA   I'll never give up my, never give up my dreams of singing. Like, that's my world. That is just my world. That's my world, yeah. I would never give that up. It's cos like, I was like eight years old and I saw loads of singers and all them stuff. And then, one day, I started to sing with my mum. And then…I had a voice!

KARL   What kind of things do you like to sing?

TAMEKA   I don't know.

KARL   Sing for us now. Come on, if you like singing. … No? Why not?

TAMEKA   I don't know.

KARL   OK, don't, I won't ask you to sing.

NADIA   I would like to live in California and Sans Francisco. It would be like a mansion and there's like a pool house and… How would, like, how do you imagine, like, your house being? Like what sort of like theme is it going to be? Things like that.

RUTH   I haven't really thought about that. I want to live in a big house, but not that big. Like that one that makes me scared, and that stuff. Like, let's say you were just by yourself at home, you would be scared, like, if like all the lights are out. I'm always scared at lights out.

NADIA   But, like, like, you know in America, um, there's this brand called Lush and they have like body stuff, there's one like when you bath yeah, when you bath yeah, um, and it's kind of like a bath one –

RUTH   Yeah.

NADIA   – when you bath in it, it makes you like fall asleep straight away.

RUTH   Oh cool! I never knew about that one.

Everyone leaves except KARL and TAMEKA.

KARL   What does it feel like when…in your house, when you can sing, and you don't need to worry about anybody listening to you? What does that feel like?

TAMEKA   …It feels like I can do anything.

12.

ZACHARY   There was a…er, I was walking, er, I was walking and then…

SID   Oh yeah, you know, this, yeah you told me…

ZACHARY   And then the, a man, he got hit by a car, and it looked like a ragdoll, and it was just lying on the floor. And I got so freaked out, I was so scared.

SID   You still don't know what happened to him?

ZACHARY   What?

SID   He, he wouldn't have died.

ZACHARY   No he wouldn't.

SID	Because…
ZACHARY	But it…was so scared…and he was just lying on the floor. And his shoes, they just flew…
SID	Mm.
ZACHARY	Like they flew like ten metres away.

13.

A high-pressure job interview.

GRACE	What are your favourite sweeties?
CAREY	Lollipop. …Liquorice. …Haribos. …That's it.
GRACE	Which one's your –
CAREY	And bubblegum!
GRACE	Which one's your favourite out of them?
CAREY	Bubblegum.
GRACE	Why?
CAREY	Because I can blow big bubble and I might be able to set the world record.
GRACE	What would you do… If you were like, like a, like this bubblegum creature, what would you do?
CAREY	I will change into different colours like one of those lizards when they're scared. And I'd pop into a big bubble to fly aways to places.
GRACE	If, if you were the bubblegum creature, and you were in a hot tub, would you melt?
CAREY	Yes. Actually no, because I would have a hard bubblegum shell.
GRACE	OK. Mm. What's your second favourite out of your, out of your favourite sweeties?

CAREY   Haribos.

GRACE   Why?

CAREY   Because I like the egg one.

GRACE   …If you were a eggy creature what would you
           do?

14.

KARL   Do you think audiences could tell that it's words
           by children, or not?

GRACE   Nnyeah, little bit.

           Cos, um, like children they, they sound a bit
           more like quieter and the adults sound a bit
           more louder.

           And, um, the adults, um, sound, um, like, like,
           if they were, like, like if they were angry at
           someone a little bit.

15.

NADIA   OK, let's talk about who we, um, like the most
           in our family.

RUTH   Ooh. Do you mean like mum or dad?

NADIA   Um… I like my mum.

RUTH   I like my mum better.

NADIA   I never liked my dad.

RUTH   I don't get to spend that…most of my time with
           my dad. He still works so I don't really know
           him like…I'm like a stranger to him because
           like…I only say hi to him, and he only knows
           that I'm his daughter, not like… We don't
           connect, we don't really have a…um, a father

and a daughter's relationship like, like a father and a daughter should have.

I used to spend most of the time with my grandmother. She doesn't live here, she lives in Ethiopia. My grandma, like, raised me up, we didn't live with my dad. After he works he only comes to see me like sometimes at night when I'm asleep, and I don't see him like most of the times. Cos when he comes, eleven o'clock and that stuff, I'm already asleep. – And in the weekend when I see him he's asleep! *(Laughs.)* When I'm not.

NADIA   I have like… I have like a lot of stepbrothers and, um, I've got one stepsister. Cos like, my dad, he works, and like sometimes like when he… You know when somebody gets frustrated –

RUTH   Yeah.

NADIA   – they like go to the pub and drink some –

RUTH   Beer.

NADIA   – things. And then…

RUTH   Whiskey.

NADIA   …there's a woman.

RUTH   …Yeah, OK.

NADIA   Yes, I have a lot of step-… Um…

Pause.

RUTH   Brothers and sisters.

NADIA   Yeah.

16.

LAUREL   Um… I broke my arm.

I was on the monkey bars –

And I went to the medical room, and the person in the medical room said it's probably just going to be a bruise.

So I had to go back to class.

I didn't really cry. I didn't really want to cry, because… I don't know.

But I do hurt myself lots now.

Because I play rugby.

I'm the only girl.

It's kind of lonely.

(Whispers.) I do like it.

17.

KARL   So you have two brothers and one sister, is that right?

LAKEISHA   *Five* brothers. And one sister.

KARL   Ah!

LAKEISHA   Just wish it was the other way round.

KARL   Why do you wish it were the other way round?

LAKEISHA   Because boys are silly, and girls are not silly. Cos in the boys' toilet, they're always so noisy, cos there's always there's loads of them, they're always so noisy and noisy. But when the girls are in the girls' toilet, they don't shout, they just… they just do what they're doing and then they come out peacefully.

KARL   *(Laughs.)* Why do you think boys are noisier than girls?

LAKEISHA   Because boys… *(Sigh.)* …have this kind of, um…lively action where they…where they're silly. They have the silly feeling in them. And girls just have this calm feeling in them, where… Because they think straight and they don't have silly answers or things like that.

KARL   Let me try this out. Can we talk about…girls?

HASSAN   No!

KARL   Are you interested in girls?

WOODY   No!

HASSAN   No! Except for my mum and my sister. And my cousin. No one else.

KARL   OK. So do boys and girls kind of play separately in your year?

HASSAN   Sometimes. But most of the time they play girls catching boys –

WOODY   Yeah.

HASSAN   – which is just wrong.

WOODY   …It is kind of fun though.

HASSAN   Yeah. But it's wrong. Trust me.

RACHID   Basically, yeah, basically they're, they're like "Ewwww, ewwww, look at my nails."

OMAR   And yeah, and yeah, they fight like this…

RACHID   Yeah like catfight basically. That's the only difference. And they kick weak.

KARL   And what?

RACHID   They kick weak.

OMAR   Eh, eh, eh, eh, eh, cos, girls, cos, cos, cos the girls will smack you in your face!

RACHID   Yeah, right! That's the true bit!

OMAR   Yeah.

RACHEL   Right. What do you think about boys? – Ugh! …Sorry.

CRESSIDA   Well some boys can be a bit…gross.

RACHEL   Yeah like there's this boy that we know and he goes to our school and he's really weird. He like sings to his jelly. And I find that a bit odd. And then when the boys are telling us we're weird!

CRESSIDA   And they like pick their nails.

RACHEL   I know! It's smank!

CRESSIDA   *(Whispers.)* Smank!

RACHEL   And they like think they're so good at football and all that.

CRESSIDA   I know.

RACHEL   It's like… Yeah. It's just… Not nice, really.

KARL   OK, OK. So let's not talk about that then.

HASSAN   No.

18.

On a bench in the park.

ZACHARY   And that's – that's one of the things that I think about, is like, what is up with our generation? What is up with it? I mean it's just a bit weird. I mean what is happening to children?

SID   They act like they are from Essex. Like one day they all did their hair all over and they acted like…

ZACHARY   Oh my gosh.

SID   Sometimes… I see them out on the street
            sometimes.

ZACHARY   Yeah, I do, I do.

SID   And they look like utter chavs.

ZACHARY   I mean it's just like to show off.

SID   Boys and girls. Showing off together.

ZACHARY   And when I think about that it's just like, Why?
            Seriously. I mean if you think back to the
            1960s…

SID   Well we weren't alive, obviously.

ZACHARY   Or the… Yeah, I know, but if you think back…
            And the 1970s… The girls weren't at all like they
            are today.

SID   Yeah because girls now are like chavs. Mostly.

ZACHARY   Whereas, like, in the…early days, they were just
            like playing with bubbles. Just running around.

SID   *(Laughs.)*

ZACHARY   There's one girl in our class who like… OK.
            Today she was wearing like the shortest skirt
            ever.

SID   You just thought: That's the sort of thing that
            22-year-old girls wear.

ZACHARY   It's so short. It was literally like…ten centi-…no,
            slightly bigger, maybe twenty centimetres, the
            skirt.

SID   Yeah.

ZACHARY   In length. And I was just like –

SID   From the shoulders all the way down.

ZACHARY   …No, no, it was just, it was just the skirt.

SID   Yeah it was just…, yeah.

ZACHARY   Inappropriate!

SID   Inappropriate clothing! Exactly!

ZACHARY   I mean it's inappropriate when you're older and
                   inappropriate now. It's even more inappropriate.

SID   I mean I see a couple of, um, girls walking down
                   the street and they're in our year, and I saw
                   I think one person from secondary school, in
                   about sixth form, and he's looking at her literally
                   like she was a object. And that girl actually –

ZACHARY   Liked that.

SID   – liked that, yeah. Which I thought was a bit
                   shocking.

ZACHARY   And I'm just like: Why? Seriously.

SID   Anyway.

ZACHARY   It's just disappointing. They should just improve!

SID   Yeah our generation should just generally
                   improve.

ZACHARY   Yeah. …I mean the boys are all right. But the
                   girls, they act… Too mature. Like, over-mature.

SID   There is a absolute huge difference between the
                   boys and the girls.

ZACHARY   Yes. – And I think what's happened is that the
                   generation of girls…

SID   – has completely changed.

ZACHARY   …has just gone down and down, as in like…

SID   …going around literally mugging people… And
                   there are people our age, um, younger than us
                   by about probably a couple of months, um, in
                   the riots, involved in the riots.

ZACHARY   Yeah there was a girl who was in the riot.

SID   There were loads of girls –

ZACHARY   In the riots. Why? I mean not even boys should be doing that.

SID   No, nobody should be doing that.

ZACHARY   It's just terrible.

SID   You cannot get away from going outside because otherwise you'll get rickets. So…

ZACHARY   Rickets?

SID   …Er… lack of the sun.

ZACHARY   OK.

SID   You cannot escape from the outside. Because otherwise you get ill and stuff. And now, whenever you go outside, you're scared of being mugged, raped or killed.

ZACHARY   Yeah, well.

SID   Because now they're telling you, oh no, the crime rate has gone up.

ZACHARY   "Thank you! That's really going to help me!"

SID   We don't need to know that. Because now we're just going to be even more scared. You're trying to terrify us –

ZACHARY   Exactly.

SID   – out of our homes. …Terrify us *into* our homes. – Apparently this is the safest time to be a child. I don't think it is, actually. Because if you think about it, we've got, um, all those mugging things going on.

              Quiet.

              Er… Yep. So that was a good conversation.

19.

KIM   Cake.

A cake.

It's very creamy and it's very soft and it has lots of flavour on the top.

It's a circle cake... And it's very tall... And it has a cherry on the top. And it has a design, it has a, because it's a wedding cake.

And when you eat it it's delicious.

You have to spend lots of money to buy a wedding cake.

And... It has lots of jam inside it.

And in the middle...

There's a little bit of chocolate and jam inside.

When you cut it in half you can see chocolate and jam, when you cut it a half again you can see some little flowers inside it.

...And I've finish.

20.

A game of pétanque.

WOODY   Once I was with my dad, and we was playing 'The Legend of Zelda: Majora's Mask'. It's a really hard game, and I knew what to do but my dad wouldn't listen to me. So I said, Dad, Dad, I know what to do, can I have a turn? And he just kept on ignoring me. So when I finally got a turn, I got five minutes and then it was dinner time. And then I had to turn it off!

HASSAN …Wait, can I quickly just turn up a subject?
– Um… Divorceness. Have you, have your
parents ever been divorced?

WOODY Er, my parents aren't married, they are
boyfriend and girlfriend.

HASSAN Oh OK. You mean divorced.

WOODY Yeah, not like Henry the Eighth divorced his
wife, no. They've had arguments, like real
punching *(Laughs.)* and kicking. And they've
also like *(Laughs.)* took the Hoover thing to them
and then a metal thing to them…

HASSAN Ouch!

WOODY *(Laughs.)* It was OK. They didn't hit as hard as
they should of. And once when I was young,
what I did was, when my, when dad, my dad
was beating up my mum, I gave, I gave my
mum, I gave my mum the umbrella! Which had
a metal thing at the end. *(Laughs.)*

HASSAN *(Laughs.)* …Yeah my parents argue but they
never divorce. I think it's never good to divorce
because I mean look. You go to one place and
then the next. And then… *(Coughs.)*

WOODY God bless you.

HASSAN And then… – Thank you. – And then, at the
end, your parents both want you to marry, um,
two different women.

WOODY Yeah, my parents, when they get mad, they like,
after their argument and their fight which is
normally about me –

HASSAN *(Laughs.)*

WOODY *(Laughs.)* – er, they, my dad normally goes
to his house and stays there for the night and
comes back in the morning all refreshed saying,

like, sorry. And once I like watched this film
and it's about this family and they don't get
along, and in a section, they leave the youngest
sister behind, and they leave her on the bench
because the mother and the grandmother, they
take so long trying to find their underpants.

21.

ADAH   Well, when I'm angry, like, I try not to show it to
people, so that I don't make them sad and make
them worry about me.

Cos sometimes when I go to school, like, I'm
angry for some reason, cos sometimes I just feel
like I should be angry when I shouldn't.

So then when I see my friend, like she just talks
to me and then cheers me up, and I forget about
that I was even angry, or upset.

Like when I'm angry I don't talk much to
people, I just listen to what they say, and not say
anything.

And I don't really like it when I'm angry
because I upset my mum and she has a long way
to go to work.

So I'm going to try not to, um, be angry or
upset. And when other people are angry I'll try
and encourage them, like how my friends did it
to me.

22.

MATTHEW   Um, I've been a mascot for a rugby team, and I
had to go on, um, go on the Twickenham turf.

KARL   With a crowd there?

MATTHEW   Yeah.

KARL   How many people were there?

MATTHEW   Um, I think it was 61,000.

Um, the scariest bit… Cos all the players walk out, um, just like in football. Um, but when you have to turn round and sing the national anthem. Because you've got to face the crowd and…everyone's…like, looking straight at you, and I, I had to try and, um, block out all the crowd and just try to find my dad. Cos that was, like, my reassuring point.

Um… I, I knew around about where he was sitting.

It's just I couldn't find him exactly.

I think it's made me a lot less scared of loads of people looking at me. I'm still scared of other things.

Um…

Well, I have a fear of when my parents die.

Um…

KARL   It's all right.

Quiet.

MATTHEW   *(Whispering to himself.)* What else, what else? Um…

Quiet.

Yeah, I've got my, um, great-grandparents still alive.

Um, he's ninety-nine this year. He's…his mind is still in really good con…tact. So, um…

We thought that we, for his a-hundredth
birthday, we'll get him some tickets to the
Olympics.

23.

A busy urban pub. Talking over music.

KARL   How does the government get money? What
do they do? They get their money from us… So
it's…

TRAYVON   Yeah but our taxes go to the Olympics, though.

KARL   Not all the taxes!

TAMEKA   But why are they *mean*? Why do they have to
take money from us?

KARL   Where else are they going to get money from?

TAMEKA   They're the government, they can print bare
loads of money.

TRAYVON   They, they, they can stop buying stuff!

KARL   Where do they get the money from though?

TRAYVON   Fake money, they can print, they can print it off
the internet.

TAMEKA   You see, yeah, you see, yeah, when you park a
car and then it's not in the right place you get a
ticket. When you pay the money it goes to the
government.

KARL   Exactly.

TAMEKA   But if you do it in the Queen's parking space
then it goes to the Queen.

TRAYVON   The Queen, if you park in the wrong place, they
will crunch your car up.

TAMEKA   It's like, it's like we're the Queen's prisoners or
            something like that.

TRAYVON   But the royal Qu-, the royal family, yeah, they
            just show off, yeah, that's why if the Queen was
            walking down the road with no guards, someone
            gonna beat her up, cos…she got loads of money
            and stuff. She got jewels on and everything.
            That's why some people don't like royal
            families. Cos they show off with their money
            and they like just take taxes away from other
            people.

TAMEKA   I do like the Queen. I hate some royal family,
            like… Sometimes I don't really like Kate
            Middleton, but…that's people like us, that's
            what they think.

TRAYVON   Our money's going to them, like, they're, they're
            buying their jewels.

TAMEKA   I do like Prince William, I do like Prince Harry,
            and I do like Charles, I do like Princess Anne, I
            do like the Queen.

TRAYVON   But our money's going to their…their jewels and
            stuff. So, why don't they sponsor us any money?
            They just sponsor the thingy.

TAMEKA   The jewels are for free. The jewels are…

TRAYVON   But how do, how do they make the jewels
            without no money?

TAMEKA   You dig up the ground! And you find bare real
            gold.

TRAYVON   But they pay people to dig up the ground!

TAMEKA   You find real gold in the ground.

TRAYVON   But they pay people to dig up the ground. So
            our tax is still going to them.

TAMEKA   No, some people just have brains, and just dig
          up the ground.

          Cut to:

STEVIE   My dad gave me a twenty pound yesterday.

KARL   Did he?

STEVIE   Yeah. He gave me a twenty pound.

JAMAAL   Well, well I have more than that.

STEVIE   My mum has fifty pounds and my dad has
          twenty pounds and ten pounds and five pounds.
          And he's so rich! He has like one hundred and
          six hundred pounds.

KARL   My goodness me.

JAMAAL   Well I have more than that. I have like, I just
          have like, um, money like just like a mountain.

KARL   Really?

JAMAAL   Yeah bigger than this whole school.

KARL   Seriously? You have a mountain of money at
          home?

JAMAAL   Yeah.

STEVIE   Well I'm going to bring my twenty pound
          tomorrow.

KARL   OK.

JAMAAL   And then you can put your twenty pound on
          top.

KARL   OK. If, just im-, if, like, an alien came down
          from another planet –

STEVIE   Yeah?

KARL   – how would you explain to them what money
          was?

JAMAAL   I would be like, money is… I'll be like this: Can
          you see these little things? He's gonna be like:
          Yeah? And I'm gonna be like: It's money.

          Cut to:

KARL   Do you think it's exciting having the Olympics?

TRAYVON   It's a waste of time! It's just so people can get
          famous and go in the Guinness World Record
          for doing something. It's hard to get in the
          Olympics so people just showing off cos they
          got…they can do running with no legs and stuff.

TAMEKA   No I like the Olympics. You can just support
          your country and be proud of that.

          Cut to:

CRESSIDA What's your favourite country?

RACHEL   *(Laughs.)* Oooh. Actually… I guess England,
          because…

CRESSIDA Yeah me too.

RACHEL   It's where I belong.

CRESSIDA Because I'm proud to be British.

RACHEL   Yeah. And like yeah.

CRESSIDA I mean who isn't?

RACHEL   Mmm.

CRESSIDA Who isn't? Because we've helped so many
          people in like countries in war. So like… In like
          World War 2, we, um, helped… The Americans
          helped us, and…

RACHEL   Yeah.

CRESSIDA Sometimes we're helping them.

RACHEL   That reminds me like proud of the Queen. Shall
          we sing 'Diamond Queen'?

CRESSIDA No.

24.

A therapy session. JACK is under hypnosis.

KARL   Do you ever have scary dreams?

JACK   Yeah, once I had one.

KARL   What was your scary dream about?

JACK   Falling down from the Empire State Building.

KARL   …All the way down?

JACK   Yeah. From the very very top.

KARL   And was it one of those dreams when it feels like it's actually happening?

JACK   Yeah. Once I, once I felt like I was tipping, I was tipping forward when I had that dream. And luckily it wasn't scary cos I landed on the soft mat.

KARL   So you actually landed…in the dream?

JACK   Yeah.

KARL   On a soft mat.

JACK   Yeah.

KARL   At the bottom of the Empire State Building!

JACK   Yeah I landed in the dream.

KARL   And then did you wake up straight away, or…

JACK   Yeah. I waked up straight away.

KARL   What happened when you woke up?

JACK   I…

KARL   What was that like?

JACK   I shouted out to my mum.

KARL   Of course.

JACK   Yeah.

KARL   And told her about the dream.

JACK   Yeah. Falling down from the Empire State
              Building.

KARL   …All the way down?

JACK   Yeah. From the very very top…

The scene repeats in a loop. Overlay:

WOODY   Every time I'm naughty, I alway-, I, I always just
              use, I, I, I, I got my, I got my cousin to teach me
              like little fake crocodile tears. So *(Laughs.).* So I
              put my head down and say "OK, I'll just go in
              my room" and they fall for it every time! And
              they let me play it, they let me continue play
              and they don't tell of me or anything. *(Laughs.)*

WOODY's speech also repeats. Overlay:

KARL   Count down from ten till one for me. …So start
              from ten.

JACK slowly coming out of his hypnotic state.

PHOEBE   Ten.

LAUREL   Nine.

PHOEBE   Eight.

LAUREL   Seven.

PHOEBE   Six.

LAUREL   Five.

PHOEBE   Four.

LAUREL   Three.

PHOEBE   Two.

LAUREL   One.

PHOEBE   Zero!

WOODY stops speaking. JACK opens his eyes.

25.

KARL	What makes you angry?
GRACE	Um… When sometimes when, when people don't listen to me or like they don't give me what I want! *(Laughs.)*
KARL	What's that like, when people don't listen to you? How does that feel?
GRACE	I feel like…like I'm in this world with…that no one, that no one, um, that I'm the only one in that world. Like there's no one else.
KARL	Mm. And what do you do when it's like that? How do you get people to listen to you?
GRACE	I… I just shout at them, or I just, um, go like that. *(Smacking herself.)* Wake up wake up!

26.

A political husting.

KARL	*(From the audience.)* If you could change one thing in the world, if you could change *one thing*, what would it be?
HASSAN	Hmm…
WOODY	…What I would change is…
HASSAN	OK you go first.
WOODY	I would change people who steal, I will turn them into nice people. And people that, that like are nice people, even more nice people. Like, even nicer.
HASSAN	Why did you choose that?
WOODY	I chose that because look outside. There are crooks everywhere. Who wants a place with crooks when you can have like nice people

always in the sunshine flying kites about? Not people who *steal* kites! We want a nice place of earth. Not where people spit their chewing gum on the floor.

HASSAN   OK. Mine is a really interesting one.

WOODY   And what would that be?

HASSAN   Um, if I could change one thing in the whole world, I'd change how many, um, things I can, I can have, because then I can have more than one thing.

WOODY   I thought you was going to say you would have superpowers or something.

HASSAN   Yeah that's what I was going to say! And then the first thing I would have is all the superpowers in the world.

WOODY   So you would have Spiderman's?

HASSAN   Mm… Yeah. All the superpowers.

WOODY   Green Lantern's?

HASSAN   Yes!

WOODY   Basically, if you had all the, all of them, no offence but you would also have Ben 10's.

HASSAN   …Nah, I would just throw away all the rubbish ones.

27.

KARL   Just imagine that you were allowed to run the country for like a year.

SULAIMAN   Yeah.

KARL   What things would you do? What would you do about money, in particular?

SULAIMAN   Well, um, we'll save it, probably, we'll save it
            to give to other people, like, um, for, for people
            that come from, like, um, countries like Algeria
            and Africa. Cos like some people don't have
            money and, well, some people are rich. Cos
            like... Say like the conflict, the, um, violence in
            Syria right now.

            I always watch it, like, the Syria violence. I
            watch it either on the news on the internet,
            anything. Cos, um, I need to. I'm a Muslim, so
            I watch it cos I know that I'm... I was trying
            to support my religion. All I see is like saying
            people have been killed in this violence and
            stuff. Cos all around the world, in all Muslims'
            country, there's, like, all violence, like Libya's
            violence, like Gaddafi being killed and stuff.

            Cos you know, um, the, um, God, Allah?

            When I was reading the Qu'ran, um, when I was
            finished, I saw at the back it said: Allah loves
            war. So then I said: no wonder that every time
            we have a war, in every Muslim country like
            Libya, Syria, Afghanistan, and stuff like that,
            Sudan... I started to watch the news cos I knew
            that, um, my God loves war, so I'm gonna watch
            it, cos we all know that he loves war, so cos he
            loves war...there's a war going on now in any
            country, in any time.

            Cos sometimes, like, I pray to him with my dad
            sometimes. But like when my leg's hurting and
            stuffs, um, I don't, because like, when I bend
            down to, um, like, put my forehead on the
            mat, my leg starts to pain cos like, um, my leg's
            crampling, and then when I go like this, it's like
            my, um, I'm being hitted on the forehead with a
            baseball ball.

I don't like really spend money on sweets and stuffs. I just spend money on giving it to, um, countries that like… There was this thing saying, Save… Save Ghana for money. And then I just put it in.

28.

CRESSIDA   Um… Why do you think we have wars?

RACHEL   Because… Um… Um… I don't actually know, like… I think people should stop now because, game over, you know?

CRESSIDA   Yep. *(Quiet but hysterical giggles.)*

RACHEL   …Yeah.

CRESSIDA   It's a bit annoying. …So I don't think there's any…thing…more to really talk about.

RACHEL   Yeah.

CRESSIDA   I suppose.

RACHEL   You know, life's good really. How's your life?

CRESSIDA   Good.

Silence.

RACHEL   Um…

CRESSIDA   So…I suppose it…because…I don't know. Do you have any other questions?

29.

ALICE   When you're a child you don't really think…cos you like to live like a child.

Doesn't really seem you're just going to be an adult

like time flies by and you just want…to, like, stay as a child,

but you just enjoy things, the way it goes.

30.

KARL   OK. Well listen, it's been very nice to have a conversation with you. Has that been OK?

ELINA   Yeah.

RACHEL   Yep.

KARL   Been all right?

RACHEL   Have you been recording this?

KARL   Well yes! Cos the little red light's on there, so it's all been recorded. …Did you say anything that surprised you?

Everyone starts packing up and leaving.

RUTH   Um… I usually don't talk that much. I get really shy, like.

NADIA   At first I didn't want to do this cos I thought that, like, you were going to take, like, um, a video of us. And then sometimes like people just like put it on the internet like what Mr Ogilvy done.

RUTH   Yeah. I always think, I don't think the good thing about the people, I only think about the bad thing of it. I'll be like, what if they're judging me like? I think that everyone's judgey. And I've come to learn that not everyone judges you, like.

OMAR   Bye bye everybody!

KARL   How was that, was that all right?

HASSAN   Yep.

WOODY   Yeah.

KARL   Do you get a chance to just talk to each other? When do you get to talk?

HASSAN   No we don't.

WOODY   Er, like, kind of at the end of the day.

HASSAN   No but we never get a chance. That's the thing. I never get to know Woody and Woody never gets to know me. And like… And I want you to hear this loud, world! That is why we're not friends! Because we can never get to know people.

And I think… And if you… And if you can hear this, President, I want you to change the school time so that we can have play time even more so we can know people even more. OK? …Please can you –

WOODY   Make more maths! Make more maths!

HASSAN   *(Laughs.)*

KARL   OK. Cool. Thank you very much. …Is there anything you want to ask me? I want you… I want it to feel fair.

KIERAN   No, not really.

DEXTER   No.

KIERAN and KARL go, leaving DEXTER alone on stage.

Oh, I do have one question. – How does it feel like, being an adult, just in general?

Fade to black.